My Wee Granny's

Old Scottish Recipes

Plain, delicious and wholesome

Scottish fare from my

Wee Granny's table to yours

Angela Hossack

Dedicated to my Wee Granny

Annie Clark

1890 - 1971

Contents:

Base Stocks

Soups

Fish Dishes

Catsups, Stuffing and Sauces

Poultry

Game and Other Meat Dishes

Bridies and Pies

Vegetable Dishes

Puddings and Tarts

Bannocks and Scones

A word about Shortbread

BASE STOCKS

You can't make a good pot of soup, a rich gravy, a good stew or a curry without a good, rich base stock. Traditionally, stockpots were on the go all of the time – simmering away over the fire or on the stove with bones and leftovers continuously replenishing it. These days, some home cooks tend to use stock cubes or simply make the stock as they go along preparing and cooking the dish. My wee granny always had base stocks prepared in advance. I follow in her footsteps and tend to either make my stock the day before I need it or make a huge pot and freeze it.

In these busy times, soup-makers may resort to stock cubes (and it's not a sin to add the odd stock cube or two to your stockpot) but you can't beat the genuine article. Gravies, soups, stews, or curries made with only stock cubes tends not to have the full body or the flavour of a home-made stock; so, wherever possible, get your stockpot simmering.

The most important thing to remember about a good stock is that it needs time… hours and hours of time, but you don't have to stand over it and watch it. You can leave it alone. Just throw your bits and pieces in the pot, cover with water, put a tight lid on and leave it alone for at least four hours, but preferably longer.

Something else that's important… keep and freeze every chicken, turkey, duck carcass; every trimming from any meat you've used to cook with; save the lamb bone from the leg you have on Sunday; keep beef bones, ox tail bones and pork bones. Waste nothing… including skin and fat. Freeze it until you need it.

If you haven't used the juices from a roast for gravy – don't discard – keep for your stockpot.

And, what about the outside celery stalks that you tend to discard, or the stalks of broccoli and cauliflower? The outside leaves and stalks of cabbages? The leftover raw or cooked vegetables? Yes, you've guessed it – throw in the stockpot. Just make sure everything is washed under cold running water first.

As you work your way through my wee granny's recipes, you will see that I make reference to a base stock in many of the dishes. If you – like my wee granny did, and as I do now – have the base stock already prepared then the cooking of the dish will be much quicker than making your stock at the same time as you make the soup.

Your basic **vegetable stock (V)** – scrubbed carrots with their skins left on, the outside celery stalks that you tend to discard, a couple of whole onions, the outside leaves and the end root of the leek, or a whole leek if you have one going spare, cabbage, broccoli and cauliflower stalks, leftover raw and cooked vegetables and a whole garlic bulb.

Put everything in a pot with water, put it on to boil, cover with a tight lid, simmer and forget about it. When it's simmered for at least four hours, discard the veggie bits and pieces and season to taste with salt, pepper, celery salt and onion salt.

I use **Chicken stock** a lot. We eat a lot of chicken in our house and my freezer is usually crammed with carcasses. I have a stock pot that can take up to 8 carcasses.

I don't bother defrosting the carcasses, I just cover with water, bring to the boil and simmer under a tight lid for at least 6 hours. I give it a stir now and again, otherwise I leave it alone and get on with other things. Straining can be a bit of a pain, but it's worth it.

Season to taste with salt, pepper, celery salt and onion salt.

You only actually get about 3 pints of stock from 8 carcasses, but you can imagine how rich and delicious it is. I put the stock in a large bowl, cover and allow to cool. It then goes in the fridge overnight and the fat is removed in the morning.

You can, of course, make smaller amounts of chicken stock. If I know that I want stock for a gravy, or a curry or a small pot of soup the day after I roast a chicken, then I immediately get the carcass on to simmer. A single carcass is simmered for about 3 hours and I get just under a pint of stock.

Mixed meat stock – made with any or all of your yummy lamb, beef, ox tail and pork bones you have to hand, as well as any meat trimmings or any leftover cooked or uncooked meats. Cover with water and bring to the boil. Remove all the scum that forms on the top (this will ensure a nice clear stock).

Gently simmer for as long as you can, but for at least 4 hours. Season to taste with salt, pepper, celery salt and onion salt.

Strain and leave to cool then put in the fridge overnight so that the fat solidifies on top and then skim.

Rich beef stock is a bit more expensive to make because it doesn't just rely on bones and trimmings. Hough (shin) and brisket are the staples for a good, rich beef stock along with the beef bones and trimmings, but the meat can then be used for a variety of dishes. Make your beef stock as you would a mixed meat stock *but don't bring it to a rolling boil*…. bring it to a gentle simmer. After it has simmered for 3 hours, remove the joint of shin and the joint of brisket and then continue simmering the bones and trimmings for at least another hour – preferably longer. Season to taste with salt and pepper.

Your rich beef stock can be enhanced with the addition of ox tails or you can make a pure **Ox tail stock.** Ox tails are delicious and you can use the meaty bones afterwards. Make you ox tail stock as you would a mixed meat or beef stock, remembering to skim off the scum when it comes to the boil. Season to taste with salt and pepper.

A favourite stock of my wee granny was a simple **vegetable, brisket and breast/neck of lamb stock.** This stock formed the basis of many soups and stews. To the ingredients of the basic vegetable stock, add a joint of brisket and the breast of lamb and follow the method for making the rich beef stock, removing the brisket and the lamb after 3 hours. Season to taste with salt, pepper, celery salt and onion salt.

The lamb breast and/or neck can then be used, for example, in Scotch Broth and the brisket for sandwiches or a number of dishes.

Smoked or unsmoked ham stock is the basis for lentil soup, pea and ham soup and other dishes you will find recipes for later on in the book. You need celery stalks, a large leek, a large onion, a couple of carrots and a smoked or unsmoked gammon or ham hock and/or cuts of smoked or unsmoked bacon. Cover with water and bring to a slow boil. Remove the scum formed on the top and simmer for 3 hours. Season to taste with salt, pepper, celery salt and onion salt. Cool and leave in fridge overnight and skim and discard the fat that has congealed on the top.

Basic fish stock – fish heads and bones fried for a few minutes gently in butter alongside a roughly chopped onion, 2 stalks of roughly chopped celery and roughly chopped stalks of parsley. Season with celery salt, thyme, a bay leaf, salt and pepper then put in your stock pot, add a cup of white wine to every litre of water and simmer for one hour. Strain through a sieve. For a **richer shellfish stock** use the heads and shells of prawns, lobster shells, razor fish shells and the strained liquor of mussels and follow the method for your basic fish stock but cook out for an additional 30 minutes.

SOUPS

A good soup takes time but, because you've already spent the time making your stock, the actual soup takes much less than an hour. If you start your stock and your soup from scratch it can take up to five hours so, best to prepare your stock the day before if possible.

Everybody has their own version of how to make soup. The following recipes are the versions I grew up with in Scotland. They were handed down from my wee granny (my great grandmother), to my granny, to my mum and to me. Some of the recipes date back to the early 1900s.

Quite a few – if not most – soups of Scotland are filling enough and nutritious enough to stand, with a slice or two of crusty bread, as a main meal.

Scotch Broth

Serves 6 - 8

Preparation: pre-soak the broth mixture (a half of a cup of pearl barley, a third of a cup of split yellow peas and a third of a cup split green peas). Pre-soak overnight in cold water.

Prepare your stock. For Scotch Broth use the vegetable, brisket and lamb stock recipe.

What you will need:

1.5 litres of stock

Either the meat from the lamb or the brisket (Scotch Broth can include either beef or lamb)

Pre-soaked broth mixture – (64g of pearl barley, 64g of yellow split peas and 64g of green split peas)

2 large onions

4 large carrots

2 white turnips

Small swede

A head of celery

A cup of chopped curly leaf parsley (128g)

What you need to do:

Add the pre-soaked broth mix to the stock and bring to a slow boil. Simmer for forty minutes, stirring occasionally.

Chop up the brisket **or** pull the lamb.

Chop and dice the onions, carrots, turnips and celery and add to the pot. Continue to simmer for a further fifteen minutes then add most of the parsley and your chosen meat and simmer for a further five minutes.

Remove from the heat and garnish with the remaining parsley. Add additional seasoning if required.

Cock -a-Leekie Soup

Serves 6 - 8

<u>Preparation</u>: chicken stock

<u>What you will need</u>:

1.5 litres of stock

Small chicken

8 leeks

<u>What you need to do</u>:

Bring the stock to a slow boil and add the chicken to the pot.

Wash the leeks and prepare them by cutting off the root and about an inch from the top; remove the outer leaf and cut/split lengthwise then chop into one inch lengths. Give the cut leeks a final rinse in cold water and add to the pot.

Simmer for one hour. Remove the chicken and take it off the bone and return the chicken meat to the pot. Add additional seasoning if required. Remove from the heat and serve.

Kale and Oatmeal Soup

Preparation: Vegetable stock

Serves 4

What you will need:

1 litre of vegetable stock

4 cups (chopped) Green kale (240g)

Quarter of a cup of oatmeal (32g)

Half a cup (150ml) double cream

What you need to do:

Wash and de-vein the kale and roughly chop

Bring your vegetable stock to the boil

Add the kale to the stock and simmer for one hour

Remove the kale and chop up finely and toss it in the oatmeal

Return to the pot

Gently warm the cream and add to the pot

Stir and simmer for 5 minutes

Add additional salt and pepper as required

Hotch Potch

Serves 6-8

<u>Preparation</u>:   Soak the dry peas and the broad beans in   cold water overnight. Prepare chicken, vegetable, or   mixed meat stock.

<u>What you will need:</u>

1.5 litres of stock

6 carrots

6 small white turnips

1 cup (128g) of dried peas

1 cup (128g) of broad beans

Small cauliflower

1 little gem lettuce

6 spring onions

Half a cup (65g) of curly leaf parsley

<u>What you need to do:</u>

Skin **half** of the peas and all of the broad beans and then   put half of the peas to one side

Bring stock to the boil and add the skinned peas and broad beans

Peel, cut and dice the carrots and the turnips and add to   the pot.

Simmer for 40 minutes

Meantime cut the cauliflower into florets and chop the lettuce. Cut the spring onions into small pieces. Chop the curly leaf parsley.

After the initial 40 minutes simmer, add the remaining half cup of peas, the cauliflower, lettuce and spring onions to the pot. Stir and then add the chopped parsley.

This is a thick soup but you can add more stock if you prefer it a little thinner.

Add additional seasoning if required.

Skink

Serves 6-8

Preparation: Prepare your rich beef stock and keep the shin and/or the brisket as this will form part of the dish.

What you will need:

1.5 litres of beef stock

The shin and/or the brisket used to make the stock

4 large carrots

1 small swede

2 leeks

Head of celery

2 onions

Half of a savoy cabbage

What you need to do:

Bring stock to the boil

Chop and dice the carrots, swede and onions

Chop and cut up the celery

Cut the cabbage and the leeks and chop into small pieces

Add all of the prepared vegetables to the stock and simmer for 30 minutes.

Cut the shin and/or brisket into small cubes and add to the pot.

Switch off and allow the residual heat to warm through the beef.

This is a thick soup but you can add more stock if you want it a little thinner.

Red Lentil and Tomato Soup

Serves 4

Preparation: Prepare your smoked or unsmoked (whatever is your preference) ham stock. Prepare your tomatoes by soaking in boiling water until the skins can be peeled.

What you will need:

A third of a litre of slightly salted water

1 litre of ham stock

1 cup (128g) of red lentils

4 carrots

1 onion

2 stalks of celery

4 large fresh tomatoes

What you will need to do:

Bring the salted water to the boil

Rinse the red lentils and add to the water. Cover and simmer for 20 minutes stirring frequently so as not to burn on the bottom. Add more boiling water if required.

Peel, chop and dice the carrots, onion and the tomatoes.

Remove the fibrous stringy bits from the celery and chop into small pieces.

In a separate pot, bring the stock to the boil, add all of the vegetables and simmer for 20 minutes.

After the lentils have simmered for 20 minutes leave to one side.

Once the vegetables have simmered in the stock for 20 minutes, use a potato masher to roughly mash them and then add the lentils. Stir thoroughly and simmer for a further 10 minutes.

Red Lentil and Barley Soup

Serves 6

Preparation: Prepare the brisket/lamb stock or, if you prefer you can prepare the vegetable stock. Soak the pearl barley overnight in cold water.

What you will need:

1.5 litres of either vegetable or mixed meat stock

1 cup (128g) of red lentils

1 cup pearl barley

4 carrots

1 onion

2 stalks of celery

What you will need to do:

Rinse the red lentils and the barley and add to the stock. Bring to the boil, cover with a tight lid and begin simmering.

Peel, chop and dice the carrots and onion and add to the pot.

Remove the fibrous stringy bits from the celery and chop into small pieces and add to the pot and gently simmer for one hour. Add more stock if required.

Add additional seasoning if required.

Tattie Soup version one

Serves 6-8

<u>Preparation:</u>   prepare vegetable, chicken or mixed meat stock

<u>What you will need</u>:

1.5 litres of stock

2lb (907g) of potatoes

2 onions

2 stalks of celery

Half a pint (250mls) of milk

Cup of curly leaf parsley

Tablespoon of flour

Splash of vegetable oil

<u>What you will need to do:</u>

Chop and dice the potatoes and onions, remove the fibrous stringy bits of the celery and chop into small pieces. Fry all these vegetables in the vegetable oil for 5 minutes.

Bring the stock to the boil and add the vegetables. Cover and simmer for 15 minutes then use a potato masher to mash.

Wash and chop the parsley.

Blend the flour with the milk and add to the pot to thicken. Stir well and add the parsley.

Add additional seasoning if required.

Tattie Soup version two

Serves 6-8

Preparation: prepare your rich beef stock

What you will need:

1.5 litres of rich beef stock

2lb (907g) potatoes

4 carrots

Small swede

2 leeks

Cup of curly leaf parsley

What you need to do:

Dice the potatoes, swede and 3 of the 4 carrots and add to the beef stock. Bring to the boil and simmer for 30 minutes.

Wash and cut the leek lengthways and then into small pieces and after the vegetables have simmered for 30 minutes, add the leek to the pot and simmer for a further 30 minutes.

Chop the curly leaf parsley and add it 5 minutes before serving.

Add additional seasoning if required.

Feather Fowlie

Serves 6-8

<u>Preparation:</u>   prepare your chicken stock

<u>What you will need</u>:

1.5 litres of chicken stock

Small chicken

2 slices of ham

Head of celery

2 onions

3 egg yolks

Half a cup of curly leaf parsley

A teaspoon of thyme

A dessertspoon of cream

<u>What you need to do</u>:

Joint the chicken and add it to the stock with the 2 slices of ham and bring to the boil. Simmer for 40 minutes. Remove the fibrous stringy bits from the celery and cut into small pieces. Chop and dice the onions, chop the parsley and add to the pot with the thyme and simmer for a further 20 minutes.

Remove the chicken and the ham Take the meat off the bone and cut into small pieces. Cut the ham into small pieces. Skim the grease from the stock. Remove the pot from the heat and stir in three whisked egg yolks and the dessertspoon of warmed cream. Add the chopped chicken and ham meat.

Add additional seasoning if required.

Crab Soup

Serves 4

Preparation: pre-cook 1 crab, pick out all the meat but keep the meat of the large claws to one side. Prepare your chicken stock.

What you will need:

1 litre of chicken stock

The meat of 1 cooked crab

Half a cup of rice

One cup of milk

1 cup of double cream

What you will need to do:

Boil the rice in the milk until cooked. Pass the rice and the crab meat (with the exception of the meat from the 2 large claws) through a fine sieve into a bowl. Stir and make a smooth paste then very slowly mix in the (cold) chicken stock.

Put into a pan and put on the heat. DO NOT BOIL. When hot, but not boiled, stir in the crab meat from the large claws and, just before serving, stir in the cup of double cream.

Haricot Bean Soup

Serves 6-8

<u>Preparation:</u> Soak 340g (12oz) of haricot beans in cold water overnight. Prepare ham stock.

<u>What you will need:</u>

1.5 litres of ham stock

340g (12oz) of pre-soaked haricot beans

2 onions

1 swede

450g (1lb) potatoes

1 tablespoon of flour

2 cups of milk

Half a cup of curly leaf parsley

<u>What you will need to do:</u>

Cut and dice the onions, swede and potatoes. Rinse the beans and add to the stock along with the diced vegetables. Bring to the boil and cover with a tight lid. Simmer for 2 hours then force through a sieve and return to the pot. Mix the flour with a little of the milk and stir through the soup to thicken and then add the remaining milk.

Chop the parsley and just before serving, add to the pot.

Tomato Soup

Serves 4

Preparation: prepare your unsmoked ham stock. Put tomatoes in boiling water so they can be skinned.

What you will need:

1 litre of unsmoked ham stock

8 skinned tomatoes

1 carrot

1 onion

2 tablespoons of sago

2 cups of milk

What you will need to do:

Cut up tomatoes, onion and carrot and add to the stock in a pot. Bring to the boil and add the sago. Simmer for 30 minutes. Pass through a sieve, return to the pot and add the milk. Stir and heat, but do not boil.

Dried Pea and Ham Soup

Serves 4

Preparation: soak dried peas overnight in cold water. Prepare ham stock.

What you will need:

1 litre of ham stock

225g (8oz) of pre-soaked dried green peas

1 onion

1 small white turnip

Half a cup of curly leaf parsley

Teaspoon of vegetable oil

What you will need to do:

Chop and dice the onion, carrot and turnip and fry gently in the oil then add to the stock with the peas. Bring to the boil, cover and simmer for 2 hours.

Chop the parsley for garnish

Chicken Soup

Serves 4

<u>Preparation:</u>   prepare your chicken stock.

<u>What you will need:</u>

1 litre of chicken stock

2 chicken legs

1 leek

2 large carrots

Half a cup (170g) of rice

Half a cup of curly leaf parsley

<u>What you will need to do:</u>

Put the chicken into the stock, bring to the boil and simmer for 40 minutes.

Cut and dice the carrot and add to the pot the leek lengthways and then cut into small pieces. Add to the pot with the rice and simmer for a further 30 minutes.

Add more stock if required.

Remove the chicken and take the meat off the bone and return to the pot.

Chop and add the parsley 5 minutes before serving.

Oxtail Soup

Serves 4

Preparation: Prepare your oxtail stock or use mixed meat stock that includes 8 pieces of meaty oxtail. Do not discard the oxtails as they will be added to the soup.

What you will need:

1 litre of your oxtail or mixed meat stock

8 pieces of the pre-cooked oxtail used to make your stock

3 carrots

1 swede

2 white turnips

1 large onion

Tablespoon of vegetable oil

What you will need to do:

Chop and dice the carrots, swede, turnips and onion and fry off for a few minutes in the vegetable oil.

Bring the stock to a boil, add the vegetables and simmer for 30 minutes.

Add the oxtails to the soup to warm through.

Serve 2 portions of the oxtails with each portion of soup (this was my wee granny's preferred way to serve the oxtails, as sucking out the meat from the bones was awesome, but you can fork the meat out of the bones and add it to the soup if you prefer.)

Shell Fish Soup

Serves 4-6

<u>Preparation</u>: prepare your rich shellfish stock (ensure it is well strained) Scrub and de-beard as appropriate.

<u>What you will need</u>:

1 litre of rich shellfish stock

100g Clams

100g Cockles

100g Mussels

4 Razor fish

100g King prawns

1 cup of milk

Knob of butter

Half a cup of oatmeal

<u>What you will need to do</u>:

Put all the shellfish, except the prawns, in a pot, cover with water and bring to the boil. Simmer until cooked and remove any where the shells have remained closed.

Shell and de-vein the king prawns.

Remove all the shellfish and remove from the shells. Cut up the razor fish and then add the clams, mussels and razor fish to your prepared stock. Bring back to a gentle simmer, add the half cup of oatmeal, the knob of butter and the cup of milk. After five minutes add the de-shelled and de-veined prawns. Switch off the heat, cover and let stand until the prawns cook in the residual heat.

FISH DISHES

Scotland is renowned for its abundance of fish. My wee granny most commonly cooked with herrings, salmon, trout, whiting, haddock, mackerel and cod. Many Scottish fish dishes are served with a traditional egg sauce.

Fish is low in saturated fat and low in the bad omega-6 fatty acids, high in protein and bursts with flavour. Oily fish such as mackerel and salmon are high in omega-3 fatty acids which are very good for the body.

Always ensure your fish is fresh by checking that the eyes are clear. If in doubt, place your fish in water and, if it floats, then it is fresh.

Some of these fish dish recipes date back to the 1800s and were popular during the 1900s and are still used in Scotland even today.

Please note that lard or dripping has been replaced by vegetable oil or butter.

Egg Sauce

Hard boil and chop 2 eggs. Mix 2 tablespoons of cornflour (corn starch) with 2 cups (500ml) of cold milk. Once it is smooth add 100g of butter, salt and freshly ground black pepper. Bring to the boil, stirring continuously for one minute. Blend in half a teaspoon of lemon juice, 2 teaspoons of dill and the chopped eggs.

Cabbie Claw version one

Serves 4-6

What you will need:

1lb cod fillets

1lb potatoes

2oz butter

1 dessertspoon of cornflour

Half a teaspoon of dried mustard

1 hard-boiled egg

3oz grated cheese

Half a pint of milk

Salt and pepper

What you will need to do:

Boil the potatoes until cooked then slice them

Put the majority of the milk, butter, salt and pepper into a frying pan and add the cod. Bring to a slow boil and simmer gently for 6 or 7 minutes or until the fish is cooked through.

Mix the cornflour with the remaining milk and add the mustard. Mix thoroughly and add to the pan.

Shake gently to mix through and continue shaking gently until the sauce thickens. Turn out into a casserole dish.

Place the sliced potatoes on top, add the grated cheese and put in a pre-heated hot oven for 10 minutes.

Cabbie Claw version two

Serves 4-6

What you will need:

200mls of basic fish stock

1lb cod fillets

Half a cup of curly leaf parsley

Quarter of an inch of grated horseradish

900g (1lb) potatoes

1 dessertspoon of cornflour

What you will need to do:

Boil the potatoes, cool and slice

Finely chop the parsley

Mix the cornflour with a little of the cold fish stock

Bring the remaining fish stock to the boil and reduce the heat to a gentle simmer. Add the cod and gently simmer for 5 minutes and then add the chopped parsley and the grated horseradish. Simmer for a further 5 minutes and then gently add the cornflour and thicken the stock by gently stirring (trying not to break up the cod.).

Turn out into a casserole dish and layer the potatoes on top.

Serve with egg sauce.

Traditional Whiting

Serves 4

<u>What you will need:</u>

2 cups of basic fish stock

8 whiting fillets

2 tablespoons of flour

3 knobs of butter

2 tablespoons of cream

2 tablespoons of chopped chives

Half a cup of chopped parsley

<u>What you will need to do:</u>

Ensure your fillets are dry and rub each of them with flour

Add the knobs of butter to a large frying pan, melt and add the fish and gently sauté them very slowly for 2 minutes. DO NOT brown them.

Ensure the chives and the parsley are very finely chopped and put in a bowl with the fish stock and mix thoroughly then add to the pan.

Bring to a gentle simmer and simmer for 2 or 3 minutes.

Try not to break them up when you lift them out. 2 fillets per portion

Curled Whiting

Serves 4

What you will need:

4 whole whiting with eyes removed

Half a cup of breadcrumbs

50g of melted butter

Salt and pepper

Third of a cup of chopped curly leaf parsley

Four lemon wedges

What you will need to do:

Curl each of the fish and put the tail through the eye socket.

Place in a greased tin and brush over the melted butter.

Season with the salt and pepper and sprinkle over with the breadcrumbs

Put in a preheated moderate oven and bake for 30 minutes

Garnish with the chopped parsley and the lemon wedges

Whiting Pudding

Serves 4

What you will need:

4 whole whiting

900g of potatoes (2lbs)

Half a pint (250mls) of milk

Salt and pepper

100g of butter

What you will need to do:

Boil the fish in the milk for 15 minutes

Boil the potatoes until cooked

Remove, debone and deskin

Mash the fish

Strain the milk and add 3 tablespoons to the cooked potatoes along with half of the butter. Mash and mix in the fish.

Mash the potato and fish mix to an oven proof dish and smooth out with a knife. Add the remaining butter in small dollops across the top.

Brown in a moderate oven.

Serve with egg sauce.

Traditional Herrings

Serves 4

What you will need:

8 fresh boned herring fillets (flattened carefully)

Salt and pepper

2 cups of oatmeal

Vegetable oil

What you will need to do:

Ensure the herring fillets are dry

Season with salt and pepper

Put oatmeal on a large plate and thoroughly coat each fillet with the oatmeal

Put vegetable oil in a large frying pan and heat until very hot

Add the herring and brown them until crisp on both sides

Lay on paper to drain the excess oil and serve immediately

Potted Herring

Serves 6

<u>What you will need:</u>

12 fresh boned herring fillets

Salt and pepper

12 black peppercorns

2 bay leaves

Half a cup of vinegar

Half a cup of water

<u>What you will need to do:</u>

Season each fillet with salt and pepper

Mix the half cup of vinegar with the half cup of water

Roll each fillet inside out starting from the tail end

Pack them side by side in a small pie dish and just cover with the vinegar and water mix

Add the 12 peppercorns and 2 bay leaves and bake in a preheated moderate oven

Crappit Heids (stuffed heads) (version one)

Serves 8

What you will need:

0.5 litres of basic fish stock

8 haddock heads

One cup of oatmeal

100g of butter

2 onions

One cup of white crab meat

2 anchovies

Chopped cooked yolk of 2 eggs

1 beaten egg

One cup of breadcrumbs

Salt and pepper

What you will need to do:

Chop and dice the onions and mix through the oatmeal. Add the anchovies, the crabmeat and the breadcrumbs and mix thoroughly. Break up the butter and add. Bind the mixture with the beaten egg and gently fold in the chopped egg yolks.

Use the mixture to stuff the 8 haddock heads and place them on end on the bottom of a large buttered stew pan. Cover with the fish stock, bring to the boil and simmer for 30 minutes.

Crappit Heids (stuffed heads) (version two)

Serves 8

What you will need:

0.5 litres of basic fish stock

8 haddock heads

One cup of haddock livers

One cup of oatmeal

Half a cup of milk

Salt and pepper

What you will need to do:

Chop the livers and mix with the oatmeal. Bind with the milk. Season with salt and pepper.

Stuff the heads with the mixture and place the heads on end on the bottom of a large stew pot. Cover with the fish stock. Bring to the boil and simmer for 30 minutes.

Tatties and Herring

Serves 4

<u>What you will need</u>:

0.5 litres of basic fish stock

900g (2lbs) potatoes

8 salt herring fillets

<u>What you will need to do</u>:

Peel and dice the potatoes

Put in a large pot and cover with the fish stock.

Lay the salt herring fillets on top.

Bring to a slow boil and gently simmer on a very low heat for minutes.

Spiced Salmon

Serves 4

What you will need:

4 salmon fillets

28g of salt

28g of black peppercorns

28g of cinnamon

One pint (500mls) Vinegar

One pint of water

What you will need to do:

Mix the water and vinegar and add the salt, peppercorns and cinnamon. Add the salmon fillets and bring to the boil. Simmer for 10 minutes.

Remove the salmon and allow to cool then pack them in a deep dish and cover completely with the cooled cooking liquor. Cover so the dish is airtight. Serve with egg sauce.

Salmon Fritters

Serves 4

What you will need:

4 cooked salmon fillets

450g (1lb) of boiled potatoes

Yolk of one egg

4 hard-boiled eggs

2 tablespoons of cream

Vegetable oil

Salt and pepper

What you will need to do:

Mash the boiled potatoes and mix in the egg yolk and the cream. Season with salt and pepper.

Flake the cooked salmon fillets through the mashed potatoes and mix thoroughly.

Mould into small fritters and fry in vegetable oil until golden on both sides.

Each portion to be served with a quartered hard-boiled egg.

Friar's Trout in Sauce

Serves 4

<u>What you will need</u>:

Half a litre of basic fish stock

4 cleaned and gutted whole trout

2 onions

4 cloves

4 teaspoons of black peppercorns

2 teaspoons of salt

2 glasses of white wine

4 anchovies

Juice of 1 lemon

One teaspoon of cayenne pepper

1 dessertspoon of cornflour

100g butter

<u>What you will need to do</u>:

Mix the peppercorns, salt and cayenne pepper together and divide into 4 portions. Use one portion per trout and rub the mix inside the belly of the fish. Place the fish in a stew pan and cover with the stock.

Chop and dice the onions and add to the pot. Add the 4 cloves.

Bring to the boil and gently simmer for 5 minutes and then add the 2 glasses of wine and the 4 anchovies. Add the lemon juice.

Gently simmer for 20 minutes then gently remove the trout and place in a casserole dish.

Thicken the stock with cornflour and add the butter.

Pour the stock over the trout and serve hot.

Potted Salmon

Serves 4

What you will need:

4 fillets of salmon

The juice and zest of 1 lemon

1 teaspoon of chopped dill

1 teaspoon of chopped flat parsley

1 teaspoon of cayenne pepper

200g of unsalted butter

Salt and pepper

What you will need to do:

Flake the salmon fillets and put in a bowl.

Add the lemon juice and zest, the dill and the parsley and mix. Taste and add salt and pepper to season...

Pour in three quarters of the melted butter and mix thoroughly.

Taste again and add more seasoning if required.

Divide the salmon mix between 4 teacups and smooth the tops before brushing on the remaining butter.

Chill in the fridge for 2 hours before serving.

Serve with toasted bread.

Leek and Mackerel Patties

Serves 4

<u>What you will need</u>:

450g (1lb) potatoes

2 leeks

1 tablespoon of capers

4 mackerel fillets

100g of butter

Half a cup of milk

Salt and pepper

Vegetable oil

<u>What you will need to do</u>:

Boil the potatoes in salted water and mash with the butter

Cut the leeks up very small and poach to soften in the milk season with the salt and pepper.

Add the mackerel to the milk and leeks and continue poaching until the fish is cooked through. When cooked, drain then flake the mackerel with a fork and add to the mashed potatoes. Mix thoroughly and make into small patties.

Fry the patties in the vegetable oil until golden on both sides.

Serve with egg sauce.

Crispy Skinned Mackerel

Serves 4

What you will need:

4 butterflied mackerel skin on

1 spring onion

1 lemon

Salt and pepper

What you will need to do:

Heat a frying pan until piping hot and add the mackerel skin down. Season with salt and pepper and grate the zest of the lemon over it. Fry until the skin side is dark brown – pressing down with a fish slice (for about 3 minutes) then flip over and fry for a few seconds on the other side.

Trim and finely slice the spring onions and sprinkle over the cooked fish.

Serve with buttered toast.

Crappit Cod (stuffed cod)

Serves 6-8

What you will need:

Half a litre of basic fish stock

One whole cod, cleaned, descaled and gutted

The meat from one cooked crab

4 anchovies

2 cooked egg yolks

2 eggs

1 cup of oatmeal

100g of butter

Half a cup of flat leaf parsley

What you will need to do:

Mix the crab meat, the anchovies, the oatmeal, the egg yolks, the butter and the parsley thoroughly together and stuff it into the belly of the cod.

Put the cod in a fish bath and cover with the fish stock. Cover and bake in a moderate oven for one hour.

Add additional seasoning if required.

Serve with egg sauce.

Cod and Mussel Stew

Serves 6

What you will need:

1 litre of rich fish stock

6 cod loins

500g of mussels

2 glasses of white wine

2 large potatoes

Half a cup of cream

2 onions

2 leeks

Half a cup of flat leaf parsley

Knob of butter

What you will need to do:

Cook the mussels in the white wine. Discard any that don't open after 4 minutes.

Drain and keep the liquor and add to the rich fish stock.

Peel and dice the potatoes and the onions. Clean and cut up the leek. Then gently sauté the potatoes, onion and leeks in a pan with the butter for about 8 minutes then add to the stock. Boil rapidly for 5 minutes to reduce the liquid and then add the cod loins.

Gently simmer for 10 minutes and then add the mussels and the parsley and simmer for a further 2 minutes.

Baked Cod

Serves 4

What you will need:

A cup of basic fish stock

4 cod loins

12 cherry tomatoes

2 tablespoons of flat leaf parsley

The juice of one lemon

What you will need to do:

Put the cod loins and the cherry tomatoes in an oven proof dish and cover with the fish stock. Add the lemon juice. Place in a preheated moderate oven and bake for twenty minutes.

Garnish with the parsley.

CATSUPS, STUFFINGS AND SAUCES

Walnut catsup

You need to make it in advance and keep in an airtight jar.

Ensure that your walnuts are not too hard.

To prepare before cooking - take 50 walnuts and squeeze them a little to bruise them and put in a jar with 1 tablespoon of salt and half a litre of vinegar. You then need to allow to marinade for at least a week. Y

Once marinaded, put them in a pot with a teaspoon of nutmeg, a teaspoon of cloves, a teaspoon of ginger a teaspoon of black peppercorns a cm of horseradish 10 small shallots, 200g of anchovies and 250mls (half a pint) of port.

Boil and simmer for half an hour. Taste and add more vinegar or wine if required.

You can either strain and then use the liquid or use the catsup without straining. Store in an airtight jar or bottle.

Mussel catsup

Boil 900g of mussels in two and a half cups of sherry. When the mussels are cooked, remove from their shells, mash with a potato masher and return to the cooking liquor. Add 2 teaspoons of salt and a quarter of a teaspoon of cayenne pepper and 4 anchovies. Bring back to the boil and skim.

Strain and store in airtight jars

Liquid mushroom catsup

900g (2lbs) of chestnut mushrooms, 2 teaspoons of salt, 2 bay leaves, 1 chopped onion, the zest of 1 lemon, a quarter of a teaspoon of Allspice, a quarter of a teaspoon of cayenne pepper, I tablespoon of horseradish that has been finely grated, a quarter of a teaspoon of cloves and half a cup of cider vinegar.

Carefully wipe and chop the mushrooms then put in a bowl with the salt and the bay leaves, mash them slightly with a potato masher, pat the mixture flat, cover and leave overnight to draw out the liquid.

The next day, add the chopped onion, the lemon zest, the horseradish, the Allspice, the cloves and the cayenne pepper. Stir in the cider vinegar.

Bring to the boil and simmer for 20 minutes.

Strain all the juice and put the liquid mushroom catsup it in an airtight jar or bottle.

Oyster catsup

Keep the oyster liquor and pound 16 shucked and cleaned oysters, then add the liquor and two and a half cups of sherry.

Bring to the boil, then add 2 teaspoons of salt and a quarter of a teaspoon of cayenne pepper.

Take off the boil and skim.

Strain and return to the pot and stir in a tablespoon of brandy.

Store in airtight jars.

Cucumber catsup

Slice 6 cucumber sand mix with 4 chopped onions. Add 2 teaspoons of salt, cover and leave to sit for 36 hours. Strain and add a teaspoon of chopped horseradish, the peel of 1 lemon, black pepper and a quarter of a teaspoon of cayenne pepper. Bring to the boil and simmer for 15 minutes. Strain once more and add 2 teaspoons of brandy.

Store in airtight bottles.

Basic Breadcrumb Stuffing

This basic breadcrumb stuffing forms the basis of most stuffing.

Mix 1 cup of breadcrumbs with half a cup of finely chopped flat leaf parsley. Season with salt and pepper, add a knob of butter, a teaspoon of grated lemon peel, a tablespoon of suet, a teaspoon of thyme and a quarter of a grated nutmeg. Beat 2 egg yolks and mix through thoroughly.

Liver Stuffing

Add the (chopped) liver of your choice (rabbit, chicken, wildfowl, lamb) to the basic breadcrumb stuffing. Chop one boiled egg and one rasher of chopped bacon and add to the mix.

Mushroom and Pine Nut Stuffing

To the basic breadcrumb stuffing mix, add 1 chopped onion, 4 cloves of finely sliced garlic, 500g of chopped chestnut mushrooms, 1 beaten egg and a half a cup of pine nuts.

Oyster and Ham Stuffing

To the basic breadcrumb mix add one cup of chopped pickled oysters and one cup of chopped ham.

Sage and Onion Stuffing

To the basic breadcrumb stuffing mix add 3 teaspoons of dried sage.

Haggis Stuffing

This stuffing does not use the basic breadcrumb stuffing mix.

Either use 200g of premade haggis or make from scratch.

To make from scratch –cook 1 cup of oats, and mix in chopped lambs lungs, lambs liver, lambs heart and half a cup of shredded beef suet. Chop 2 onions and add. Season with salt and pepper. And mix thoroughly.

Sweet Stuffing

1 cup of breadcrumbs, 250mls of chicken stock, 200g of butter, one and a half cups of chopped celery (remove fibrous stringy bits), 1 chopped onion, 3 chopped large sweet apples, 225 g of chopped water chestnuts (one 8oz can), 1 tablespoon sugar, half a teaspoon of black pepper.

Make applesauce from one of the apples. Bring the stock to the boil and mix all of the ingredients, put in an ovenproof dish and bake in a medium pre-heated oven until browned.

Sauce for Wildfowl version one

Bring 200mls of chicken stock to the boil and add a quarter of a cup of breadcrumbs, 3 chopped shallots, a half a glass of claret, salt and pepper. Simmer for 15 minutes.

Sauce for Wildfowl version two

A slice of bread boiled in a little chicken stock, a chopped onion, 2 cloves, a knob of butter, half a glass of white wine and a tablespoon of mushroom catsup, simmered together in a pan for 15 minutes.

Sauce for Venison version one

A simple sauce made from 2 glasses of claret that has been boiled and simmered until it reduces and becomes very thick. Add to this a tablespoon of redcurrant or blackcurrant jelly.

Sauce for Venison version two

This is a sharp sauce.

200g of sugar that has been dissolved in 250mls of champagne vinegar. Skim.

Liver Sauce for Poultry

A cup of chicken stock, half a cup of finely chopped chicken livers, 1 chopped onion, half a cup of chopped celery (with fibrous stringy bits removed), a heaped teaspoon of cornflour.

Gently fry the livers, the onion and the celery in a teaspoon of vegetable oil.

Use a little of the cold stock to mix the cornflour. Bring remaining stock to the boil and add the other ingredients. Simmer for 15 minutes and thicken with the cornflour.

Liver Sauce for Game

Follow the recipe for liver sauce for poultry but replace the stock with rich beef stock and replace the livers with venison livers. Add a chopped and gently fried rasher of bacon.

Drappit Egg Sauce

Bring 1 cup of chicken stock to the boil and fork in 2 beaten eggs. Mix in 2 tablespoons of chopped flat leaf parsley.

Oyster sauce

Shuck 250 g of oysters. Keep the liquor. Very finely chop the oysters and add to the liquid. Bring to the boil, cover and simmer for 10 minutes. Remove from the heat and add a teaspoon of salt. Once cooled, sieve and add 2 tablespoons of soy sauce.

Celery sauce

Remove the fibrous stringy bits from a whole celery, chop and add to a pan with boiling water for five minutes. Add a quarter of an inch of grated nutmeg, and season with salt and pepper. Meanwhile, put 2 tablespoons of butter and 2 tablespoons of flour in a pan, stir over a low heat until browned then add to the pan with the celery. Mix thoroughly.

POULTRY

Duck and goose should be served rare.

Chicken, pheasant, partridges and red grouse should be cooked through and not pink.

Wood grouse should be _just_ cooked – neither over or under done.

Roast Grouse

Serves 4 -6

What you will need:

2 young hen wood grouse

4 rashers of bacon

2 tablespoons of butter

A teaspoon of lemon juice

Salt and pepper

A half cup of cranberries

1 tablespoon of flour

What you will need to do:

Work the butter and the lemon juice over and inside the birds then stuff with the cranberries. Wrap the bacon around the birds and cover with greaseproof paper.

Roast in a preheated oven (moderate to hot) 30 minutes... Remove the greaseproof paper and the bacon, dust with the flour and brown in a buttered pan.

Fowl Stew

Serves 8

What you will need:

1 litre of chicken stock

1 partridge

1 small chicken

1 grouse

1 partridge

2 leeks

500g of potatoes

2 carrots

2 sticks of celery

Half a cup of flour

What you will need to do:

Joint all of the birds, dust with flour and fry until golden brown

Chop and dice the potatoes and carrots. Cut the celery into small pieces (having removed the fibrous stringy bits). Cut up the leeks into small pieces. Add the jointed birds and the vegetables to the stock, bring to the boil and then simmer for 25 minutes.

Stoved Howtowdie

Serves 4-6

<u>What you will need</u>:

500mls of chicken stock

1 chicken

250g of the stuffing of your choice

3 tablespoons of butter

10 button onions

6 eggs

Half a cup of chopped chicken livers

1 cup of chopped spinach

<u>What you will need to do</u>:

Stuff the bird with the stuffing of your choice. Place it in a stew pot that has a tight fitting lid along with the stock, the chicken livers, the onions and the butter.

Simmer gently for 1 hour. When ready mash down the livers to thicken the stock. Poach the eggs and wilt the spinach.

Serve with the poached eggs on a bed of spinach.

Pheasant Casserole

Serves 4

<u>What you will need</u>:

250mls of chicken stock

1 pheasant

1 tablespoon of flour

1 tablespoon of butter

A half a glass of claret

3 rashers of bacon

Salt and pepper

A tablespoon of chopped flat leaf parsley

<u>What you will need to do</u>:

Joint the bird and dust with flour and fry in the butter until golden brown. Put into an ovenproof dish with the stock and claret. Chop and dice the bacon then add to the dish with the salt and pepper. Cover and cook in a moderate oven for 1 hour.

Garnish with the parsley.

Whisky Chicken

Serves 4

What you will need:

150mls of chicken stock

3 tablespoons of single malt whisky

4 chicken breasts, boned and skinned

250mls of double cream

125g of butter

25g of flaked almonds

4 apples

Tablespoon of flour

What you will need to do:

Dust the chicken with the flour. Melt half the butter in a frying pan and fry the breasts until they are golden brown

Sprinkle the whisky over the breasts, add the chicken stock, cover and simmer for ten minutes. 180 degrees centigrade

Peel the apples and cut thickly into slices and, without stirring, cook in the remaining butter until partly soft.

Remove the breasts and add gently stir in the cream without boiling. Taste and add more whisky if required. Add the almonds and pour the sauce over the chicken and garnish with the sliced apples.

Roastit Bubbly-Jock

Serves 6

What you will need:

3.5kg (8lb) turkey

One cup of basic breadcrumb stuffing

300g of chicken livers

250g of sausage meat.

60g of melted butter

Tablespoon of redcurrant jelly

2 cups of warm water

What you will need to do:

Preheat the oven to 180 degrees centigrade

To the basic stuffing mix, add half of the chicken livers and the sausage meat and mix thoroughly.

Stuff the turkey cavity with the stuffing mix and ensure it is well sealed by skewering the opening.

Put the turkey in a deep dish, brush on the melted butter and add the warm water and the remaining chicken livers

Put the turkey in the oven uncovered for 20 minutes then cover with foil. Roast for 20 minutes per pound plus an additional 20 minutes.

When cooked, allow to stand for 10 minutes, meantime place the pan juices and the livers into a pan and boil vigorously until it reduces by half and add the redcurrant jelly and use as the sauce for the turkey.

Chicken Heather

Serves 4

What you will need:

1 chicken

Half a cup of melted butter

125g of clear heather honey

100g of French mustard

1 clove of chopped garlic

Quarter of a teaspoon of turmeric powder

Quarter of a teaspoon of cumin powder

Quarter of a teaspoon of chilli

What you will need to do:

Preheat the oven to 190 degrees centigrade

Place the chicken in an ovenproof dish

Mix all the other ingredients together and pour over the chicken. Cover and roast for 1 hour. Uncover and thoroughly baste the chicken with the juices and roast uncovered for another 30 minutes.

Pan Fried Pigeon

Serves 4

What you will need:

4 skinned pigeon breasts

250mls of chicken stock

2 tablespoons of red wine 1 onion

2 sticks of celery

4 slices of black pudding

1 tablespoon of butter

1 teaspoon of redcurrant jelly

What you will need to do:

Joint the pigeons

Melt the butter in a pan and add the pigeon breasts. Fry for 2 minutes on each side then remove from the pan and rest.

Deglaze the pan with the stock and the wine and add the redcurrant jelly. Reduce by half.

Meantime fry the black pudding and serve with the pigeon and the sauce.

Pheasant with Cider and Bacon

Serves 6

<u>What you will need</u>:

2 pheasants

100g of bacon

2 apples

2 sticks of celery

Tablespoon of butter

   4 sage leaves

500mls of cider

300mls of chicken stock

1 savoy cabbage

100mls of cream

Salt and pepper

<u>What you will need to do</u>:

Preheat the oven to 170 degrees centigrade

Melt the butter in a frying pan, season the birds and brown in the pan.

Put the birds in an ovenproof dish.

Chop the bacon and dice the onion. Cut up the celery (after removing the fibrous stringy bits) and cut up the sage. Add all of these ingredients to the pan and fry gently for 10 minutes, remove excess fat.

Cut up the apples and place over the pheasants.

Chop the cabbage and add to the dish with the stock and the cider. Cover and put in the oven for 25 minutes then mix through the cream.

Pot Roast Late Season Grouse with Wild Mushrooms

Serves 8

What you will need:

2 grouse

6 shallots

2 carrots

8 chestnut mushrooms

6 cloves of garlic

I cup of cream

1 pint of chicken stock

40mls of brandy

2 teaspoons of wholegrain mustard

Salt and pepper

What you will need to do:

Dry the birds and season with the salt and pepper. Brown in a frying pan with the butter and put in a large stew pot.

Chop the carrots, garlic, mushrooms and shallots and add to the pot. Pour over the stock and half of the brandy. Half cover with a lid and bring to the boil then gently simmer for 25 minutes.

Remove the birds and further reduce the stock. Add the cream and the mustard and reduce still further. Add additional salt and pepper if required. At the last minute, add the remaining brandy.

GAME AND OTHER

MEAT DISHES

Pickled Pork

Pickled pork is usually used as a seasoning meat, but you can also pickle leg, rump or shoulder and then roast. This recipe uses either pork hocks or belly pork.

What you will need:

4 pork hocks or 1200g of belly pork

1 and a half litres of cold water

1 litre of vinegar

4 teaspoons of black peppercorns

3 bay leaves

4 teaspoons of whole coriander seeds

30g of sugar

400g of salt

2 onions

What you will need to do:

Wash the pork and put in a large stew pot with all of the ingredients except the pork. Bring to a rapid boil and simmer for 10 minutes. Skim off any scum that forms on the top. Rapidly cool the liquor by sitting the pot in iced water.

Trim the pork of excess fat and place in a larger airtight container. Pour over the cooled liquor ensuring the pork is fully submerged. Keep in the fridge for 3 days.

Once pickled and cured, the pork can be cut up and used as a seasoning for other dishes (for example – see Kingdom of Fife Pie recipe) or can be roasted.

Square (Lorne) Sausage

What you will need:

450g of minced beef

450g of minced pork

50g of minced pork fat

150g of pin head rusk

Half a cup of cold water

2 teaspoons of salt

One and a half teaspoons of black pepper

One and a half teaspoons of ground coriander

Half a teaspoon of grated nutmeg

What you will need to do:

Combine the minced beef, minced pork and minced pork fat.

Mix the salt, pepper, coriander and nutmeg and mix thoroughly through the meat. Add the water and mix through once more then mix in the rusk.

When fully mixed, put in a loaf tin and cover. Put in the fridge for 24 hours, turn out of the tin and slice.

Fry the slices for 2 to 3 minutes on each side.

(Can also be used for stovies)

Aberdeen Sausage

What you will need:

450g of Lorne sausage meat

450g of minced beef

4 rashers of bacon

1 cup of fresh breadcrumbs

1 beaten egg

Salt and pepper

Half a cup of toasted breadcrumbs

What you will need to do:

Chop the bacon finely.

Mix together the sausage meat, the minced beef, the bacon the cup of fresh breadcrumbs. Season with the salt and pepper and bind with the beaten egg.

Mould the mixture into a roll and wrap it in a floured muslin cloth then boil for 1 and a half hours.

Remove from the cloth and roll in the toasted breadcrumbs.

Serve cold.

Roast Haunch of Venison

Serves 6

Preparation: season the venison by rubbing a mix of salt and black pepper all over then soak it for 6 hours in a mix of 500mls of claret or port and the juice of 3 lemons. Turn and baste frequently.

What you will need:

1 haunch (back leg) of venison around 3kg in weight

2 tablespoons of butter

1 teaspoon of walnut catsup

1 tablespoon of flou500mls of rich beef stock

What you will need to do:

Once you have marinaded the meat, strain the liquor.

Melt the butter and rub into the haunch.

Cover with greaseproof paper and roast in an oven pre-heated to 220 degrees centigrade for 20 minutes and then turn the oven down to 150 degrees centigrade and roast for 10 minutes per half a kg to serve rare. 15 minutes before it is ready, remove the greaseproof paper, baste thoroughly and dredge lightly with flour until it froths and browns then add the stock and the catsup ketchup to the roasting pan and leave in the oven for the remaining 15 minus.

Venison Collops

Serves 6

<u>What you will need</u>:

Haunch, neck or loin of venison cut into slices

500mls of rich meat stock thickened with flour and butter

200mls of claret

Tablespoon of butter

<u>What you will need to do</u>:

Bring the stock to a gentle boil and add the claret.

Fry the collops in butter until lightly browned on both sides

Pour the sauce over the collops and serve

Hare Casserole

Serves 4

<u>What you will need</u>:

1 hare (young)

4 rashers of bacon

2 tablespoons of butter

60g (2oz) of flour

500mls of mixed meat stock

3 onions

1 bay leaf

A teaspoon of peppercorns

2 glasses of port

<u>What you will need to do</u>:

Joint the hare and cut the bacon into strips. Chop and dice the onions.

Melt the butter in a frying pan and brown the hare and fry off the bacon. Put into an oven proof dish. Add the stock and stir in the flour, the peppercorns and the bay leaf.

Cover tightly and cook in a slow (low) oven for 3 hours. After 3 hours, stir in the port. Keep the lid off and continue in the oven until the sauce thickens.

Tighnabruaich Rabbit Stew

Serves 4

Preparation: wash the rabbit and soak overnight in slightly salted water.

What you will need:

1 rabbit

30g (1oz) of flour

500mls of mixed meat stock

2 onions

3 carrots

Salt and pepper

1 tablespoon of butter

What you will need to do:

Joint the rabbit

Cut and dice the onions and carrots

Season the flour with salt and pepper and coat the joints of rabbit.

Coat the rabbit with the flour and fry in the butter with the carrots and the onions until browned.

Place in a stew pot, cover with the stock and bring to a slow boil. Simmer until tender.

Scots rabbit Curry

Serves 6

What you will need:

750mls of mixed meat stock

2 rabbits

6 slices of streaky bacon

4 onions

4 cloves of garlic

A teaspoon of grated ginger

A tablespoon of grated coconut

A teaspoon of cumin

A teaspoon of ground coriander

Half a teaspoon of dried chilli powder

Half a teaspoon of turmeric

A quarter of a teaspoon of cayenne pepper

A tablespoon of flour

Half a cup of cream

2 tablespoons of butter

A teaspoon of lemon juice

What you will need to do:

Chop the rabbits up into pieces, chop and dice the onions and chop the garlic and add to the butter in a pan. Brown in the butter and add the stock with the flour, the coconut, ginger, cumin, coriander, cayenne, turmeric and chilli.

Cut the bacon up and add to the pot, cover and simmer for half an hour then add the cream and simmer for a further 10 minutes.

Stew and Dook

Serves 6-8

This stew is **not** served browned nor thickened.

What you will need:

1 litre of rich beef stock

1200g (3lbs) beef hough (shin)

250g of minced beef

3 beef kidneys

6 onions

What you will need to do:

Remove the fat from the hough (shin) and cube

Chop and dice the onions

Cut the kidneys length ways and remove as much of the fat gristle from the middle. Chop.

Bring the stock to a gentle boil and add the cubed hough, the minced beef, the diced onions and the kidneys.

Simmer very gently for 3 hours and add additional salt and black pepper if required

Serve in a bowl and then dook (dip) in your bread

Stovies with Lorne

Serves 4-6

What you will need:

900g (2lbs) of potatoes

6 sliced Lorne sausage

6 onions

Salt and pepper

Tablespoon of butter

Half a cup of water

What you will need to do:

Peel and cube the potatoes and cut and dice the onion. Cut the Lorne sausage into cubes.

Gently fry in the butter for 2 minutes and then add to a non-stick pot with the half a cup of water seasoned with the salt and pepper.

Cover very tightly and simmer on a very gentle heat for 1 hour. Try not to stir too much so as not to break up the potatoes and be very careful with the heat so that it doesn't burn or stick to the bottom of the pan.

Minced Beef Collops

Serves 6

<u>What you will need</u>:

450g (1lb) of minced beef steak

1 tablespoon of butter

2 onions

250mls of rich beef stock

Tablespoon of oatmeal

<u>What you will need to do</u>:

Melt the butter in a pan

Chop and dice the onions and fry in the butter for 2 minutes then add the minced steak and mix well to prevent the mince from forming lumps.

Add the stock, cover and simmer for 1 hour. Add the oatmeal and cook for another 2 minutes.

Auld Reekie Steak

Serves 4

<u>What you will need</u>:

4 fillet steaks

1 cup of cream

4 tablespoons of Scotch whisky

125g of grated smoked cheese

25g of butter

Salt and pepper

<u>What you will need to do</u>:

Fry the steaks to your liking

Meantime flambé the whisky then add the cheese and the cream. Simmer gently until reduced by half. Stir in the butter and season with the salt and pepper. Pour over the steaks.

Oxtail Stew

Serves 4

What you will need:

500mls of rich beef stock

1 whole ox tail

2 carrots

2 onions

1 tablespoon of flour

I tablespoon of butter

What you will need to do:

Chop and dice the carrots and onions.

Remove excess fa and cut the ox tail into joints. Dip in the flour and brown in a pan with the butter. When brown remove the meat and add the carrots and onions and fry gently for a few minutes and then return the ox tail to the pan. Add the stock and simmer for 3 hours.

Potted Hough

Serves 6-8

<u>What you will need</u>:

1200g (3lbs) of beef hough (shin)

1 beef knee or knuckle bone

Salt and plenty of black pepper

<u>What you will need to do</u>:

Remove the fat from the hough (shin) and cube

Put the beef and the bone in a stew pot, cover with water and season with salt and pepper

Bring to a gentle boil and then simmer for 6 hours

Remove bone and meat, discard the bone and finely break up the meat with a fork. Return it to the pot and ensure it is covered by the water it was cooked in – adding more water if required...

Return to the boil and simmer for a further 10 minutes.

Leave it to cool and then press into a mould or a deep dish. Put in the fridge and served sliced, cold.

Pan Cooked Gigot and Barley Broth

Serves 6

What you will need:

1 gigot (leg) of mutton

4 carrots

6 white turnips

2 onions

1 litre of your vegetable, brisket and lamb stock

Half a cup of pearl barley

What you will need to do:

Put the gigot in a large stew pot and add the stock. Bring to the boil and skim. Simmer gently for 1 hour then add the barley and simmer for a further half an hour.

Chop and dice the carrots, turnip and onions and add to the pot. Simmer for a further hour.

Stuffed Lamb Shoulder

Serves 4- 6

<u>What you will need</u>:

1 boned and butterflied shoulder of mutton

200g of your basic breadcrumb stuffing

Sauce (the sauce for venison version one goes very well with this dish)

<u>What you will need to do</u>:

Lay the shoulder flat, skin side down and spread the stuffing over it. Roll as tight as you can and tie with string. Put in a roasting tin and into a pre heated moderate oven for 15 minutes per kg.

Lamb Chops with Marmalade

Serves 4

<u>What you will need</u>:

4 leg of lamb chops

75mls of vinegar

75mls of mixed meat stock

4 tablespoons of marmalade

60g of butter

Salt and pepper

<u>What you will need to do</u>:

Fry to brown the chops in the butter

Season with salt and pepper. Add the vinegar and the stock. Put a tablespoon of marmalade on top of each chop and cover tightly with a lid and simmer gently for 45 minutes.

Pork and Cream

Serves 4

<u>What you will need</u>:

1 pork filet

1 cup of cream

1 tablespoon of butter

2 cloves of garlic

6 chestnut mushrooms

Salt and pepper

1 teaspoon of wholegrain mustard

<u>What you will need to do</u>:

Cut the fillet into medallions and brown in a pan with the butter.

Chop the mushrooms and the garlic and add to the pan. Toss and gently fry for a minute. Add the cream and the salt and pepper.

Simmer gently uncovered until the cream reduces then stir in the mustard and simmer for a further minute.

BRIDIES AND PIES

Different pastry is used for different bridies and pies. Shortcrust pastry, hot water pastry and puff pastry are used.

Shortcrust pastry – 225g of plain flour, 100g of butter, pinch of salt, 3 tablespoons of water.

Cut the butter into cubes. Sift the flour into a bowl and rub in the butter until the mixture resembles fine breadcrumbs. Mix in the salt and the water and knead slightly and wrap in cling film. Put in the fridge to cool.

Hot water pastry – 500g of plain flour, 175g of lard, 225g of water, pinch of salt and a little milk for glazing.

Sift the flour and the salt into a bowl. Heat the lard in the water and put it into a well you create in the flour. Mix thoroughly.

Rough puff pastry – 250g of strong plain flour and 250g of butter. Pinch of salt. 3 tablespoons of water.

Cut the butter into cubes. Sift the flour into a bowl. Add the salt and the cubed butter. Using your fingertips, rub in the butter slightly but do not go as far as breadcrumbs. The butter should remain visible in the mix. Make a well in the mix and add the water. Mix and forma ball. Put in cling film and put in the fridge.

When you roll out the dough ensure you don't work the butter too much. Roll it until the pastry is 3 times the original width.

Minced Beef Collops Round

Serves 4

What you will need:

Shortcrust pastry

Rough puff pastry

Cooked minced beef collops

Milk for glazing

What you need to do:

Roll out the shortcrust pastry and line a greased 22cm round pie tin. Pierce the pastry with a fork and blind bake until cooked.

Add the cooked minced collops mix.

Rollout the rough puff pastry and top the pie. Score and glaze with the milk. Bake in a pre-heated hot oven. Turn the pie around in the oven after 10 minutes and cook for another 5 minutes.

Forfar Bridies

Serves 3

<u>What you will need</u>:

900g of shortcrust pastry

900g of topside steak

Half a cup of shredded suet

1 onion

Salt and pepper

Milk for glazing

<u>What you will need to do</u>:

Cut and dice the steak into small pieces and season with the salt and pepper.

Chop and dice the onion and add it to the steak.

Divide the pastry into 3, roll out thinly into an oval shape. Cover half the pastry with the steak and onion and top with shredded suet.

Fold and using water, crimp around the edges. Slice a hole in the top and glaze with milk.

Bake in a hot oven for 30 minutes.

Venison Bridies

Serves 3

Make as for Forfar bridies, replacing the steak with breast of venison cut small and adding 100mls of rich beef stock to moisten the meat.

Scottish Mutton Pies

Serves 3

<u>What you will need</u>:

900g of hot water pastry

900g of lean mutton

1 onion

250mls of the vegetable, brisket and lamb stock

2 teaspoons of cornflour

Milk to glaze

<u>What you will need to do</u>:

Knead the pastry on a floured board until smooth. Remove a quarter of the pastry to keep for the lids. Cut the pastry into 3 pieces and mould it around the bottom of a glass to shape.

Chop and dice the onion. Cut the mutton into small pieces and mix with the onion. Use a little of the stock to moisten and share the mixture between the 6 pastry cases. Use the remaining pastry for 6 lids. Cover each of the pies with lids, wetting the edges and cut a hole in the top.

Glaze with the milk and bake in a moderate oven for 40 minutes.

Meantime mix the cornflour with a little of the stock. Bring the remaining stock to a boil and stir in enough of the cornflour to thicken.

When the pies are done, pour a little of the gravy in through the hole on top of the pies.

Kingdom of Fife Pie

Serves 6

What you will need:

900g of rough puff pastry

1 rabbit

900g of pickled pork

100mls of rich beef stock

Half a cup of liver stuffing

A half a teaspoon of nutmeg

2 tablespoons of white wine

Milk for glazing

What you will need to do:

Cut the rabbit into 6 pieces and soak in cold water for an hour.

Cut and dice the pickled pork and season with salt, pepper and the nutmeg.

Mix the liver stuffing with the stock to make a gravy. Put the rabbit, the pork and the gravy into a pie dish and cover with thinly rolled rough puff pastry.

Cut holes in the pastry for ventilation and bake in a moderate oven for one and a half hours.

Scottish Steak and Kidney Pie

Serves 6

<u>What you will need</u>:

2 cups of rich beef stock

900g of rough puff pastry

900g of lean stewing steak (shin is best)

450g of ox kidneys

6 beef link sausages (the seasoning in the sausages helps to season the pie filling)

Tablespoon of flour

Milk for glazing

<u>What you will need to do</u>:

Trim and dice the stewing steak and cut each beef link into 3 pieces. Cut the kidneys length ways and remove the gristle in the middle. Toss these ingredients in the flour and add to the stock. Bring to a gentle boil and gently simmer for 45 minutes then put in a large pie dish.

Rollout your pastry thinly and cover the pie filling, crimping the edges. Score with a knife and glaze with milk.

Bake in a moderate oven for 45 minutes or until the pastry is fully cooked.

Macaroni and Cheese Pie

Serves 4

What you will need:

900g of hot water pastry

350g of macaroni pasta

100mls of milk

300g of grated cheese

Teaspoon of mustard

Teaspoon of salt

Black pepper

What you will need to do:

Cook the macaroni in salted water and drain. Mix through the milk and 250g of the grated cheese. Season with black pepper. Add the mustard. Leave to stand for 5 minutes whilst the pasta absorbs the cheesy milk.

Prepare 4 pastry shells (as for mutton pies) but use all the pastry as these pies do not have lids. Bake the shells in a moderate oven until cooked through.

Fill the 4 pie shells with the macaroni and cheese. Sprinkle the remaining cheese on top and put back in the oven for 5 minutes.

Serve immediately.

A Bride's Pie

Serves 4

<u>What you will need</u>:

900g of rough puff pastry

The meat of 2 previously boiled calves' feet

450g of mutton suet

450g of sliced apples

200g of currants

200g of raisins

Half a teaspoon of ground cinnamon

Half a teaspoon of grated nutmeg

A teaspoon of candied orange peel

A teaspoon of lemon peel

1 glass of brandy

1 glass of Madeira

<u>What you will need to do</u>:

Mix the chopped calves feet meat, the suet and the apples and add the fruit, the cinnamon, nutmeg and orange and lemon peel. Mix in the brandy and the Madeira.

Line a loose bottomed pie tin with pastry and cover with the mixture. Roll out the remaining pastry and cover. Cut a hole for ventilation.

Bake in a hot oven for 45 minutes or until the pastry is cooked.

(Traditionally, a gold wedding ring was placed under the pastry lid and the top was decorated with cupids.)

Scots Potato 'Pie'

Serves 6

<u>What you will need</u>:

6 medium to large potatoes of roughly the same size

Cooked scraps of meat (whatever you have in the fridge)

1 onion

2 tablespoons of butter

1 teaspoon of cornflour

1 cup of basic vegetable stock

Salt and pepper.

<u>What you will need to do</u>:

Carefully peel the potatoes

Cut off a 3mm (half an inch) slice from the top of each potato and keep as lids.

Hollow out the centre of each of the potatoes leaving the potato 13mm thick all over.

Finely chop or mince your scraps of meat and finely dice your scooped out potato.

Part boil the onion and mix through the minced scraps of meats and your diced potato. Season with salt and pepper.

Add the cornflour to the stock and bring to a slow boil. When thickened add a little to your mix to moisten.

Stuff the potatoes with this mixture, put on the potato lids and brush all over with melted butter. Place in a well-greased baking tin. Bake in a moderate oven for at least an hour. Baste with more melted butter throughout the cooking period.

VEGETABLE DISHES

Colcannon

Serves 6

<u>What you will need</u>:

2 cabbages

3 carrots

8 potatoes

2 white turnips

2 shallots

2 teaspoons of vinegar

2 tablespoons of butter

Black pepper

Salt

<u>What you will need to do</u>:

Cut and dice the shallots and cook in the vinegar until soft.

Cut and dice all of the other vegetables. Boil the cabbage separately in salted water. Boil the potatoes, carrots and turnips together in salted water and when cooked, mash and boil in salted water until cooked. Drain and mash. Chop up the cooked cabbage and add to the other vegetables and mix through the butter with the shallots. Season with black pepper.

Kailkenny

Serves 4

What you will need:

450g of potatoes

450g of cabbage

Half a cup of cream

Black pepper

Salt

What you will need to do:

Cut and dice the cabbage and potatoes and boil in salted water. When cooked, drain and thoroughly mash. Mix in the cream and season with pepper.

Rumbledethumps

Serves 4 -6

What you will need:

900g of potatoes

900g of cabbage

2 onions

200g of grated cheese

2 tablespoons of butter

Bunch of chives

Black pepper

Salt

What you will need to do:

Cut and dice the potatoes, cabbage and onions and boil in salted water. When cooked, mash with the butter and the pepper. Cut up the chives and mix through.

Put in a pie dish and cover with the grated cheese. Brown in the oven.

Potato fritters

Serves 4

<u>What you will need</u>:

6 kidney potatoes

2 rashers of lean bacon

1 tablespoon of fine breadcrumbs

2 tablespoons of butter

Black pepper

Salt

<u>What you will need to do</u>:

Part boil the potatoes and slice

Fry the bacon and finely chop.

Beat up the eggs and mix in the breadcrumbs and the chopped bacon and dip the sliced potatoes in the egg mixture.

Fry in melted butter until golden brown on each side.

Season with salt and pepper.

Purried Neeps

Serves 6

What you will need:

1 swede

6 white turnips

Half a teaspoon of grated ginger

2 tablespoons of butter

Salt and white pepper

What you will need to do:

Cut and dice the swede and the turnips and boil in salted water. When cooked, mash with the butter and the grated ginger. Season with white pepper.

Stewed Onions

<u>What you will need</u>

12 medium onions

Half a litre of rich beef stock

Tablespoon of cornflour

Teaspoon of mushroom catsup

<u>What you will need to do</u>:

Peel the onions and add them to the stock. Boil and simmer for 1 hour. Thicken with cornflour and add the mushroom catsup.

Clapshot

Serves 6

<u>What you will need</u>:

900g of potatoes

900g of turnips

A bunch of chives

2 tablespoons of butter

Black pepper

Salt

<u>What you will need to do</u>:

Cut and dice the potatoes and turnips and boil in salted water, when cooked, drain and mash with the butter. Chop the chives and mix through with the pepper.

PUDDINGS and TARTS

Beef and Plum Pudding

Serves 6-8

What you will need:

1.5kg of shin of beef

Half a litre of mixed meat stock

Half a cup of breadcrumbs

150 of stoned raisins

150g of stoned prunes

250g of currants

Black pepper

Half a teaspoon of nutmeg

What you will need to do:

Trim and dice the shin and add to the stock. Bring to a slow boil, cover and simmer for 3 hours. Skim and strain off the liquor into a bowl. Add the and mix thoroughly then return to the pot with the shin. Add the fruit and season with pepper and the nutmeg and simmer until the fruit is soft.

Almond Florry

Serves 6

What you will need:

450g of finely crushed almonds

900g of rough puff pastry

Quarter of a cup of orange flower water

8 eggs

Half a cup of cream

Half a glass of brandy

200g of clarified butter

450g of currants

2 tablespoons of sugar

A teaspoon of ground cinnamon

A half a teaspoon of nutmeg

What you will need to do:

Blanch the almonds in the orange flower water.

Separate the eggs and discard 4 of the egg whites. Beat the remaining 4 yolks with the other 4 eggs and mix in the cream, the brandy, the butter, currants, sugar, cinnamon and nutmeg.

Line a dish with half of the rough puff pastry and pour in them mixture. Cover with the remaining pastry and bake in a hot oven for 45 minutes or until the pastry is cooked.

Apple Florry

Serves 6

<u>What you will need</u>:

8 apples

900g of rough puff pastry

2 tablespoons of sugar

2 tablespoons of orange marmalade

A cup of water

A teaspoon of ground cinnamon

The rind of one lemon

<u>What you will need to do</u>:

Melt the sugar in the water. Add the cinnamon and

Peel, core and slice the apples and add to the sugar water. Simmer for 5 minutes then add the lemon rind.

Line a dinner plate with half of the pastry and cover with the apples. Spread over the marmalade and cover with the remaining pastry.

Bake in a hot oven for 45 minutes or until the pastry is cooked.

Prune Florry

Make as apple florry but replace the apples with 500g of stoned prunes and add a squeeze of lemon and a tablespoon of port.

Apple Pudding

Serves 4

What you will need:

6 apples

900g of rough puff pastry

170g of butter

4 eggs

A tablespoon of orange flower water

A tablespoon of brandy

1 teaspoon of sugar

The rind of one lemon

2 leftover plain biscuits

What you will need to do:

Peel, core and grate the apples and add the butter and beat until it resembles thick cream.

Beat the eggs and add to the mixture. Mix in the orange water, the brandy and the sugar.

Grind the biscuits and add to the mix with the sugar. Mix thoroughly.

Line a pie dish with pastry and add the mix. Cover with the remaining pastry and bake in a hot oven for 45 minutes or until the pastry is cooked.

Biscuit Pudding

Serves 4-6

What you will need:

6 leftover biscuits

2 cups of milk

4 eggs

1 cup of sugar

1 tablespoon of butter

1 teaspoon of vanilla extract

What you will need to do:

Break up the biscuits and soak in a cup of milk and stand for 10 minutes then beat in one of the eggs and the sugar. Beat in the remaining eggs one at a time.

Melt the butter and add to the mixture. Then add the remaining cup of milk and he vanilla extract.

Pour into a buttered pudding dish and put in a preheated moderate oven for 50 minutes or until a knife pushed into the middle comes out clean and dry.

Apple Puddings in Skins

Serves 6

<u>What you will need</u>:

6 apples

4 leftover biscuits

1 cup of minced suet

1 tablespoon of sugar

1 glass of white wine

A teaspoon of ground cinnamon

Half a teaspoon of nutmeg

1 tablespoon of butter

<u>What you will need to do</u>:

Do not peel the apples but use a corer to remove each of the cores.

Pound the biscuits and add the suet, the sugar. The cinnamon and the nutmeg and mix in the wine. Spoon the mixture into the apples but not too full as it will swell.

Place side by side on a greased baking tray and share the tablespoon of butter by placing a small knop on the top of each apple.

Put in a moderate oven for 20 minutes or until the apples are cooked through.

Clootie Dumpling

Serves 6

What you will need:

450g of flour

Half a cup of shredded suet

Half a cup of fresh breadcrumbs

Half a cup of sugar

1 teaspoon of mixed spice

Half a teaspoon of salt

A grated apple

1 cup of sultanas

One and a half cups of raisins

1 tablespoon of golden syrup

250mls of milk

What you will need to do:

Mix all of the ingredients thoroughly.

Scald a cloth in boiling water and dust with flour

Place the mixture on the cloth and tie securely but ensure that you leave plenty of room for the mixture to swell.

Place a plate on the bottom of a large pan of boiling water and place the pudding on top of the plate.

Boil for 3 to 4 hours, topping up with boiling water throughout.

When cooked, remove the cloth gently and dry out the pudding for a few minutes in the oven.

Currant Duff

Serves 6

What you will need:

400g of flour

1 cup of shredded suet

1 cup of currants

Half a cup of caster sugar

Finely grated rind of 1 orange

Water

What you will need to do:

Sift the flour into a bowl and stir in the suet, currants, rind and sugar.

Stir in enough water to make a medium consistency batter. Butter a pudding basin and add the mixture and steam for two and a half hours then turn onto a warm plate.

Drumlanrig Pudding

Serves 4-6

<u>What you will need</u>:

6 stalks of rhubarb

Half a loaf of bread

Sugar to taste

<u>What you will need to do</u>:

Stew the rhubarb in sugared water. Layer the bread into a greased pudding basin and add the rhubarb. Add another layer of bread and then more rhubarb. Continue layering until the dish is full. Cover with a large plate and leave for 24 hours in the fridge.

(You can make this dish with raspberries, strawberries and currants instead of the rhubarb|.)

Marmalade Pudding

Serves 4- 6

What you will need:

1 cup of breadcrumbs

2 cups of milk

2 eggs

Half a cup of caster sugar

2 tablespoons of marmalade

What you will need to do:

Bring the milk to the boil and add the breadcrumbs. Leave to cool.

Separate the eggs and beat the yolks with the caster sugar. Add the marmalade and add to the cooled mixture.

Beat the egg whites until stiff and stir gently into the mixture. Butter a pudding basin, pour in the mixture and steam for 2 hours.

BANNOCKS AND SCONES

Barley Bannocks

Serves 4-6

What you will need:

250mls of milk

Pinch of salt

1 tablespoon of butter

Half a cup of barley meal

Tablespoon of flour

What you will need to do:

Bring the milk to the boil with the butter and the pinch of salt. Stir the barley meal in quickly and stir continuously until it makes a dough.

Flour a board and turn out the dough. Roll out thinly and cut into 6 rounds.

Ideally you need a hot girdle, but a large non-stick frying pan will do. Bake on the hot girdle or the hot frying pan, turning once.

Eat hot.

Pitcaithly Bannocks

Serves 6

<u>What you will need</u>:

115g of butter

A pinch of salt

100g of caster sugar

1 cup of flour

A tablespoon of rice flour

A tablespoon of mixed peel

A tablespoon of flaked almonds

<u>What you will need to do</u>:

Cream the butter and sugar together and mix in the flour and the pinch of salt. Add the mixed peel and the flaked almonds.

Roll out into a cake about 13mm thick. Pinch the edges and place on a greased baking tin.

Bake in a moderate oven for about 30 minutes and cool on a wire tray.

Ardentinny Drop Bannocks

Serves 6

What you will need:

1 egg

500mls of milk

Half a teaspoon of baking soda

A pinch of salt

3 tablespoons of oatmeal

What you will need to do:

Beat the egg in a large bowl and stir in the milk. Mix in the baking soda and the salt, then mix in the oatmeal and stir until it forms a medium consistency batter.

Use a hot girdle or a non-stick frying pan. Grease with butter and pour in the batter in small rounds. Turn once the batter begins to bubble. They should be golden on both sides.

Sour-Skons

Serves 4-6

<u>Preparation:</u> soak a cup of oatmeal with a cup of buttermilk, cover and store in the fridge for a few days.

<u>What you will need:</u>

Your oatmeal and buttermilk mix

A cup of flour

A teaspoon of sugar

A teaspoon of caraway seeds

<u>What you will need to do:</u>

Mix the flour into the milk and oatmeal, add the sugar and the caraway seeds. Make into a soft dough, roll out and cut into rounds. Bake on the girdle or frying pan. Cook them steadily on the one side for about 5 minutes. You will see them begin to rise. Turn and give them about 5 minutes on the other side.

White girdle scones

Serves 8

<u>What you will need</u>:

450g of flour

A teaspoon of cream of tartar

A half a teaspoon of salt

A cup of buttermilk

<u>What you will need to do</u>:

Sieve the flour into a bowl and add the other ingredients to make a soft dough.

Turn out onto a floured board, roll and cut into 4.Flatten each piece into a round scone and divide these into quarters.

Flour and bake on a hot girdle or non-stick frying pan and turn when they are well risen and going brown on the one side. They should cook for about 5 minutes on both sides.

Treacle scones

Serves 6-8

What you will need:

1 cup of flour

2 tablespoons of butter

Half a teaspoon of baking soda

Half a teaspoon of cream of tartar

Half a teaspoon of cinnamon

Half a teaspoon of ground ginger

A pinch of salt

1 tablespoon of treacle

Half a cup of milk

What you will need to do:

Rub the butter into the flour and add the baking soda, the cream of tartar, cinnamon, ginger and salt. Mix thoroughly.

Melt the treacle in a little of the milk and stir into the mixture. Add just enough of the remaining milk to make a firm dough.

Turn out onto a floured board and knead lightly then roll out 3mm thick and cut into triangles.

Bake in a greased tin in a hot oven for 10 to 15 minutes.

Potato scones

Serves 6

<u>What you will need</u>:

450g of cold cooked mashed potato

Approximately half a cup of flour

A half a teaspoon of salt

<u>What you will need to do</u>:

Add the salt and the flour to the mashed potatoes and knead into a dough. Cut into 4 and form into rounds. Make 4 triangles from each round and brown both sides on a hot girdle or non-stick frying pan.

Special Potato scones

Serves 6

What you will need:

Half a cup of oatmeal

450g of cooked, mashed potatoes

Pinch of salt

2 tablespoons of flour

What you will need to do:

To the mashed potatoes, add the salt and the oatmeal and mix in the flour.

Roll out thinly and cut into triangles.

Cook on a hot girdle or non-stick frying pan, turning once and ensuring they are browned on both sides.

Clap scones

Serves 6

What you will need:

1 cup of flour

A half teaspoon of salt

Boiling water

Honey

What you will need to do:

Sieve the flour into a bowl and add the salt. Pour over as much boiling water as necessary to make a pliable dough.

Roll into very thin rounds (as thin as you can make them) and pat with flour if required.

Bake on a hot girdle or non-stick frying pan.

It is important that, when nearly cool, you pile them one on top of the other and roll them. They should not be kept flat. Store temporarily in a tea towel.

Serve with honey.

A WORD ABOUT SHORTBREADS

My wee granny only ever used one recipe for shortbread. Be it petticoat tails, rounds or fingers, she only used this recipe.

I love shortbread and I love my mum's empire biscuits made from my wee granny's shortbread recipe.

For shortbread and empire biscuits

You will need:

2 cups of plain flour, a cup of cornflour and a cup of icing sugar.

A block of butter (225g)

Caster sugar for sprinkling on top

Cream the butter and the icing sugar until it is smooth and creamy. Sieve the flour and mix in until it forms a dough.

Rest the dough wrapped in cling film in the fridge for 20 minutes.

To roll – place between two sheets of cling film and roll out quite thick for shortbread and thinner for empire biscuits.

Cut shortbread into fingers or rounds and for petticoat tails, put in a round baking tin. Prick the surface with a fork and bake in a moderate to high oven for about 20 minutes or until they are a pale golden colour.

For empire biscuits, roll out thinner and cut into rounds. Bake for less time and remove just as the biscuits are changing colour.

Put on a wire tray to cool and sprinkle the shortbread with caster sugar. The empire biscuits are sandwiched with raspberry jam and covered with icing.

Printed in Poland
by Amazon Fulfillment
Poland Sp. z o.o., Wrocław